FAKES

Ann Weil

www.raintreepublishers.co.uk
Visit our website to find out more information about **Raintree** books.

To order:
☎ Phone 44 (0) 1865 888112
▤ Send a fax to 44 (0) 1865 314091
▣ Visit the Raintree bookshop at **www.raintreepublishers.co.uk** to browse our catalogue and order online.

First published in Great Britain by
Raintree, Halley Court, Jordan Hill,
Oxford OX2 8EJ, part of Harcourt
Education. Raintree is a registered
trademark of Harcourt Education Ltd.

Editorial: Melanie Waldron and Harriet Milles
Design: Victoria Bevan, Steve Mead and Bigtop
Picture research: Mica Brancic
Illustrations: Andrew Painter and Jeff Edwards
Production: Julie Carter

Originated by Chroma Graphics Pte. Ltd
Printed and bound in China by Leo Paper Group

ISBN 978 1 4062 0677 7 (hardback)
12 11 10 09 08
10 9 8 7 6 5 4 3 2 1

ISBN 978 1 4062 0698 2 (paperback)
12 11 10 09 08
10 9 8 7 6 5 4 3 2 1

**British Library
Cataloguing in Publication Data**
Weil, Ann
Fakes. – (Atomic)
001.9'5
A full catalogue record for this book is available
from the British Library.

Acknowledgements
The publishers would like to thank the following for
permission to reproduce photographs: AKG p. **9** top
(Dreamworks/Andrew Cooper/ALBU); BBC p. **24** top;
Charles Maxwell p. **29** top; Corbis pp. **20** top, **13**, **27**
(Bettmann), **6**, **23** bottom; Fortean pp. **10**, **14** top;
Getty Images pp. **5** (Time Life Pictures), **9** bottom (Dave
Benett), **19** (Picture Post/Maurice Ambler); Harcourt
Education Limited p. **23** bottom (Gareth Boden); Mary
Evans Picture Library p. **23** top; Science Photo Library/
Victor Habbick Visions p. **14** bottom; TopFoto/Fortean p.
20 bottom; Topham Picturepoint p. **24** bottom; US Air
Force p. **29** middle (Tech. Sgt. Lance Cheung).

Cover photograph of a games show host holding bundles
of banknotes reproduced with permission of Getty
Images/Digital Vision.

The publishers would like to thank Diana Bentley,
Nancy Harris, and Dee Reid for their assistance in the
preparation of this book.

Every effort has been made to contact copyright holders
of any material reproduced in this book. Any omissions
will be rectified in subsequent printings if notice is given
to the publishers.

Contents

Some words are printed in bold, **like this**. You can find out what they mean in the glossary. You can also look in the box at the bottom of the page where the word first appears.

WHAT IS A FAKE?

A fake is something that is not what it seems to be. People can be fakes by pretending to be someone or something they are not. Fakes are meant to trick people. Some fakes are against the law, while other fakes are just funny jokes.

Only pretending!

Milli Vanilli was a popular music act in the 1980s. The good-looking pair won "Best New Artists" at the 1989 **Grammy Awards** in the USA.

During a live performance later that year, their backing tape started to skip, and then it stopped altogether. Everyone saw that the two men were not really singing! In 1990 it was revealed that they were hired to **lip-sync** songs recorded by other artists.

Grammy Award	award given for outstanding achievement in the recording industry
lip-sync	pretend to sing by moving lips to match the singing in a recording

Fake Fact!

The Victoria and Albert Museum in London has a whole gallery of fakes!

Milli Vanilli's Grammy Award was taken away.

This article about the giant appeared in a popular magazine in 1869.

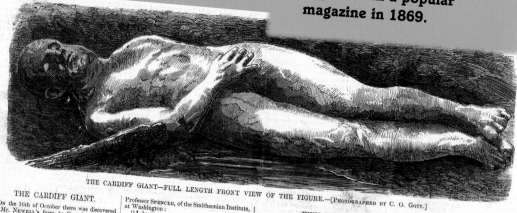

THE CARDIFF GIANT—FULL LENGTH FRONT VIEW OF THE FIGURE.—[PHOTOGRAPHED BY C. O. GOTT.]

THE CARDIFF GIANT.

ON the 16th of October there was discovered on Mr. NEWELL'S farm in Onondaga County, New York, and about thirteen miles south of Syracuse, what was at first supposed to be a petrified human form—a giant of the olden time. The first reports of this discovery excited the greatest interest among all classes, and especially among scientific men. The fossil was found about three feet below the surface while some persons were digging for a well. The soil was a sort of bluish clay mixed with quicksand and black loam, and organic remains were found about the body. The figure, when first discovered, lay in a very easy and natural position, horizontal, partly on the right side, with the right hand resting over the abdomen. Its dimensions are as follow: From crown of head to hollow of foot, 10 feet 2½ inches; crown of head to tip of chin, 1 foot 9 inches; length of nose, 6 inches; width of nostrils, 3½ inches; width of mouth, 4 inches; point to point of shoulder, 3 feet; point of hip to knee-joint, 3 feet; diameter of calf of leg, 9½ inches; diameter of thigh, 1 foot; length of foot, 1 foot 7½ inches; width of palm, 7 inches; diameter of wrist, 5 inches. The veins, eyeballs, muscles, tendons of the heel, and cords of the neck were all fully disclosed.

As we have said, this figure was at first supposed to be a petrified human form. But it was soon found that this theory seemed hardly plausible. Though the figure had the appearance of stone, the outer surface could be shaved off with a knife without dulling the blade. Dr. J. F. BOYNTON visited the figure, and, after a careful examination, pronounced it to be a statue of a Caucasian. The features were finely cut, and excellent artists have remarked the symmetry of proportions characterizing the whole figure.

Dr. BOYNTON at first supposed that this statue was carved by the Jesuits who dwelt in this valley between 1520 and 1760. After a more thorough examination he declares it to be of gypsum, and of recent origin. He says, in a recent letter to

Professor SPENCER, of the Smithsonian Institute, at Washington:

"I have stated that I thought his 'origin years;' but I am not certain that the known principles of chemistry will justify me in asserting that the period between his burial and resurrection was over three years. Its antiquated appearance has been produced not by abrasion, as many have said, but by the dissolving action of water, which, I think, could have been accomplished in a few months. A more careful and accurate calculation, admitting the possible chance of some undiscovered error creeping into the calculation, may show the burial to have taken place about 370 or 371 days ago—as it may have happened between two days."

Mr. NEWELL, upon whose grounds the statue was found, is said to have disposed of it for $40,000. The figure has been carried to Syracuse. Its weight is 2990 pounds. If it were solid stone it would not weigh so much by 500 pounds. A recent theory has been started, that it is a cast-iron figure covered with a coating of cement. The head, it is said, gives a ringing sound when struck, like that of a hollow, metallic body. But Mr. PALMER, the sculptor, states that there are marks of sculptor's tools.

EXERCISE.

INACTION weakens the body, work strengthens it. The first brings on premature old age, the second prolongs youth—that is to say, as in every thing else, in moderation. The structure of man and his mental nature show that he was not created for inactivity. Almost all those who are quoted for longevity led a more or less active or laborious life. Exercise accelerates assimilation, and with an accelerated assimilation, or process of loss and restoration, the body undergoes a more prompt and complete renovation. The secret of longevity, according to Dr. Noirot, lies in

THE CARDIFF GIANT—SHIPMENT OF THE STATUE TO SYRACUSE.—[PHOTOGRAPHED BY C. O. GOTT.]

this fact. If women live to a good old age, notwithstanding their sedentary habits, Tisset says this is to be explained by the want of bodily exercise being compensated for by their talking so much. Women are, however, much more lively and cheerful than men, and the most trifling incidents abstract their attention from more serious matters—a state of mind highly conducive to longevity. The most simple, most natural, and most beneficial kind of exercise is walking on foot. Such walks should, as far as possible, be in the open air, and in the morning. No one who can enjoy the use of his legs can, however, envy

those who take their so-called exercise in carriages. They obtain the benefit of fresh air and light, but they lose that reinvigoration of the organs, that stimulus to the vital forces, and that increase of warmth which is obtained by foot and horse exercise.

SLEEP.

SLEEP, which is a kind of anticipation of death, is in lifetime a death which restores vitality. It procures the happiness of being born again every day. The better the sleep, the greater the probability of longevity. Night ought to be consecrated to sleep. This is a law of nature which can not be infringed with impunity. Nothing is more prejudicial to longevity than devoting the nights to intellectual or bodily labors. Many literary men, learned men, and artists have died young in consequence of this practice. On the other hand, early rising, after being refreshed by sleep, is as beneficial as late work is the reverse. The amount of sleep necessary for reinvigoration depends upon the age, habits, and constitution of the individual. A new-born infant would perish if kept awake for twenty-four hours. Sleep is even more necessary after mental than after bodily labor. A man who thinks little is always in a kind of torpor. Old age, again, requires less sleep than youth and adult age. As the body is more accessible to deleterious influences at night than by day, the air ought also to be fresh, and the supply plentiful. The stomach should not be loaded. The bed should not be too soft, and, if possible, the head should lie to the north, the feet to the south. The head should never be covered by the clothes; but there should be more outer clothing at night than in the daytime, the temperature of the body not being so high. It is a good thing, on taking off one's day clothes, to lay aside also all thoughts of the past. It is only thus that complete relaxation of the mind, as well as of the body, is secured, and without this unbending of the mental faculties perfect sleep is impossible.

THE CARDIFF GIANT—FORESHORTENED VIEW OF THE

THE CARDIFF GIANT

In the 1860s a man named George Hull paid stonecutters to carve a stone giant. Then, he had it buried on a friend's farm in Cardiff, New York, USA. This "Cardiff Giant" was discovered in 1869 by workers digging a well.

A giant joke!

Some people thought it was a human **fossil**. Others thought it was an **ancient** stone statue. The public paid to view the incredible find.

But when scientists examined the stone, they realized that it was not old at all. It had merely been a prank.

Fake Fact!

The circus owner P. T. Barnum made a copy of the Cardiff Giant. Then, Barnum claimed that his copy was the "real" Cardiff Giant and the other one was the fake!

ancient   very old

fossil   animal or plant remains

FAKE PILOT

Frank Abagnale wanted to fly around the world for free. He found an airline pilot's uniform and used a fake ID card. Then he turned up at the airport and said he needed a ride.

Flying high!

For two years Frank pretended to be a pilot. He was so convincing that everyone believed him. Luckily he was never actually asked to fly a plane!

Finally, Frank was caught. He was arrested and put in prison for five years. But in 1974, Frank was released in exchange for helping police learn how to spot fakes. Now Frank helps fight crime instead of committing it.

Fake Fact!

Frank Abagnale wrote a book about his life of crime. It was made into the film *Catch Me If You Can*. The film describes itself as "The true story of a real fake!"

Leonardo DiCaprio plays Frank the "pilot" in the 2002 film *Catch Me If You Can.*

Today Frank (left) works with the police and gives talks on crime prevention.

The girls' fairy photos created a sensation around the world.

THE COTTINGLEY FAIRIES

Sixteen-year-old Elsie Wright and her ten-year-old cousin, Frances Griffiths, lived in Cottingley, England, in the early 1900s. One day they told Elsie's parents that they saw fairies down by the brook.

Fake photos

Elsie's father did not believe them and teased them about it. So, Elsie borrowed his camera and took photos of the fairies!

Elsie's father still did not believe the girls. But Elsie's mother showed the photos to some of her friends, who believed the pictures proved that fairies were real. Then someone wrote an article about the Cottingley fairies. It created a sensation around the world.

Sixty years later, Elsie and Frances confessed it was all a prank and the fairies were simply cardboard cutouts.

QUIZ SHOW

In 1956 a TV quiz programme called *Twenty-One* went on the air in the United States. It had big money prizes, but the questions were hard and many viewers found the show boring.

Giving the game away!

Then the **producers** decided to secretly give some **contestants** the answers to questions before the programme. Returning champions made the programme much more exciting to watch.

The programme became very popular. Then one of the contestants admitted he had been given the answers. Viewers were angry.

Fake Fact!

Dwight D. Eisenhower, the president of the United States at the time, called the *Twenty-One* scandal "a terrible thing to do to the American public".

Contestants had to act as if they were thinking hard about the questions.

contestant	someone who takes part in a competition or game
producer	person who organizes the business side of a programme or film

This famous photo of the
Loch Ness monster is a fake.

This is how some people think the
Loch Ness monster might look.

The Loch Ness Monster

In 1934 a man named Christian Spurling built a model of a sea monster using a toy submarine. Then, someone took a photograph of the model in the water of Loch Ness, a lake in Scotland.

Missing monster

This photograph showed a swimming creature that looked like a dinosaur with a long neck and a small head. People saw it as proof that the Loch Ness monster was real!

Finally, in 1993 Spurling confessed his role in the fake. But many people still believe the monster exists!

Fake Fact!

In 2003 researchers used sonar to search the lake. They found no traces of any monster.

sonar   using sound waves to find things underwater

THE GREAT MOON HOAX

In 1835 a US newspaper called the *New York Sun* published an incredible story. It told about life on the Moon!

Bats and unicorns

The report said there were big red flowers on the Moon. There were also purple pyramids, blue unicorns, and "man-bats" that looked like people with wings! For six days the newspaper published more of this story. Sales of the newspaper soared.

There is no doubt that the story was faked. Still the newspaper never admitted it was all a **hoax**.

astronomer	someone who observes and studies the planets, stars, and space
hoax	trick to make people believe something is real when it is not
telescope	device that makes faraway objects look closer and larger

The story said that a British **astronomer** saw strange life on the Moon by using a big **telescope**.

PILTDOWN MAN

In 1911 Charles Dawson began to find old bones in a gravel pit in Piltdown, England. He claimed they were the oldest human bones ever found. Scientists and the public were amazed.

Funny bones

Forty years later, scientists discovered that the Piltdown Man **fossils** were not that old. Some bones had been stained to look older, while others had come from different animals. The skull was from a human, but the jawbone was from an **orang-utan**.

So who was behind this **fraud**? It was probably Dawson himself, but nobody knows for sure.

No more fossils of the Piltdown Man were found after Dawson's death in 1916.

fraud	crime where someone fakes something on purpose to get fame or money
orang-utan	large ape

In 1953, scientists were able to show that the jawbone belonged to an ape.

Fake Fact!

Even scientists believed the fraud. The Piltdown Man went on display at the Natural History Museum in London in 1912.

Orson Welles was stunned by the reaction to his radio play.

CLASSICS *Illustrated*

Featuring Stories by the World's Greatest Authors

No. 124 15¢

THE **WAR** OF THE **WORLDS**

By H. G. WELLS

The radio play was based on H. G. Wells's book *The War of the Worlds*, written in 1898.

Orson Welles's "War of the Worlds"

Orson Welles was a Hollywood actor and director. He had a radio programme in the 1930s. Back then people listened to the radio for news and entertainment in the same way we watch TV today.

Scary!

On 30 October 1938, Welles and a group of actors told a **science fiction** story for Halloween on their radio programme. The radio play was written to sound like a real news report about **Martians** landing in New Jersey, USA.

Many listeners believed the report was really happening, and they were terrified! Some tried to hide from the Martians or left their homes to escape. Police emergency telephone lines were swamped.

Martian	imaginary creature from the planet Mars
science fiction	made-up story or fantasy that takes place in the future

The Fake Chess Machine

In 1769 a man claimed that he had invented a machine that could play chess. It was a cabinet with a chessboard on top. The machine seemed to move the pieces by itself and rarely lost a game.

Your move

People paid money to see the machine play chess against a real person. Before each game, a man opened the cabinet to show that there was no one inside.

The machine toured the United States in the 1820s. But it was a fake. There really was a chess champion hidden inside who operated the machine.

This poster shows "The Turk", as the great chess machine became known.

Fake Fact!

In 1997 chess champion Garry Kasparov played against a real chess-playing supercomputer called Deep Blue. Kasparov lost.

The TV programme explained how it took years of work to produce perfect spaghetti that was all the same length.

This model of a spaghetti tree was made to **commemorate** the hoax.

SPAGHETTI TREES

On 1 April 1957, British TV aired a report about people growing spaghetti. A film showed families picking spaghetti from trees.

Spaghetti harvest

The TV station got hundreds of phone calls about the programme. Many people were fooled. They wanted to know more about spaghetti trees. But it was really a big April Fools' Day joke!

Some people were angry. They thought it was wrong to make this **hoax** look like real news.

Fake Fact!

Some callers asked how to grow a spaghetti tree! Operators told them to put a "sprig of spaghetti in a can of tomato sauce and hope for the best".

commemorate   in memory of something

FAKE CAVEMEN

The Tasaday people of the Island of Mindanao in the Philippines made headlines in the 1970s. Articles and TV films reported that Stone Age people had been found still living in caves. Then the government of the Philippines said no one was allowed to visit them anymore.

Acting the part

Years later, with a new government in the Philippines, a Swiss scientist visited the "cavemen". He discovered that the cavemen were really farmers from another tribe living in huts close by. In daytime they pretended to be cavemen, but at night they went back home to their huts.

Two of the cavemen told how a government official had given them money to pretend to be part of a Stone Age tribe.

Stone Age	time long ago when people used stone tools before they discovered how to make tools using metal

CHINA

TAIWAN

N
W   E
S

PACIFIC
OCEAN

PHILIPPINES

South China
Sea

VIETNAM

Sulu Sea

Mindanao
Island

MALAYSIA

0   500 miles
0   500 km

The map shows
Mindanao Island in the
Philippines where the
cavemen were "found".

The "Tasaday cavemen"
looked very realistic.

FAKE PHOTOS

Today photographs are a very popular kind of **hoax**. Digital **cameras** and computers make it easy to construct a fake photo.

Shark attack!

In August 2001 an amazing photo of a shark attacking a helicopter appeared on the Internet. Some claimed it was nominated as *National Geographic* magazine's "Photo of the Year".

But the photo was a fake. It was made using two different photographs: one of a shark **breaching** and the other of a diver dangling from a helicopter.

People fake pictures for different reasons. Some do it for money, while others do it to get attention. Some people may do it just for fun! Still, fake photos are a bit like telling a lie.

breach	when a fish or whale jumps above the surface of the water
digital camera	camera that creates images using computer technology instead of film

Put one exciting photo ...

+

... with another exciting photo ...

=

... and you get a very exciting fake!

Glossary

ancient very old

astronomer someone who observes and studies the planets, stars, and space

breach when a fish or whale jumps above the surface of the water

commemorate in memory of something

contestant someone who takes part in a competition or game

digital camera camera that creates images using computer technology instead of film

fossil animal or plant remains

fraud crime where someone fakes something on purpose to get fame or money

Grammy Award award presented for outstanding achievement in the recording industry

hoax trick to make people believe something is real when it is not

lip-sync pretend to sing by moving lips to match the singing in a recording

Martian imaginary creature from the planet Mars

orang-utan large ape

producer person who organizes the business side of a programme or film

science fiction made-up story or fantasy that takes place in the future

sonar using sound waves to find things underwater

Stone Age time long ago when people used stone tools before they discovered how to make tools using metal

telescope device that makes faraway objects look closer and larger

Want to Know More?

Books

✱ *Fakes and Forgeries*, John Townsend (Raintree, 2006)

✱ *Forensic Files: Investigating Thefts and Heists*, Alex Woolf (Heinemann Library, 2004)

Websites

✱ www.school.discovery.com/ lessonplans/programs/forgery Learn how scientists analyse handwriting and paper to detect forgeries.

✱ www.answers.com/topic/art-forgery Find out how people forge the paintings of great artists – and sometimes get away with it!

If you liked this Atomic book, why don't you try these...?

Index

Notes for adults

Use the following questions to guide children towards identifying features of recount text:

Can you find examples of temporal connectives from page 8?
Can you give an example of scene setting from page 11?
Can you find a recount of events on page 12?
Can you give examples of past tense language on page 16?
Can you give an example of a closing statement from page 28?